Religion And Psychology

William Brown

Kessinger Publishing's Rare Reprints

Thousands of Scarce and Hard-to-Find Books
on These and other Subjects!

- Americana
- Ancient Mysteries
- Animals
- Anthropology
- Architecture
- Arts
- Astrology
- Bibliographies
- Biographies & Memoirs
- Body, Mind & Spirit
- Business & Investing
- Children & Young Adult
- Collectibles
- Comparative Religions
- Crafts & Hobbies
- Earth Sciences
- Education
- Ephemera
- Fiction
- Folklore
- Geography
- Health & Diet
- History
- Hobbies & Leisure
- Humor
- Illustrated Books
- Language & Culture
- Law
- Life Sciences
- Literature
- Medicine & Pharmacy
- Metaphysical
- Music
- Mystery & Crime
- Mythology
- Natural History
- Outdoor & Nature
- Philosophy
- Poetry
- Political Science
- Science
- Psychiatry & Psychology
- Reference
- Religion & Spiritualism
- Rhetoric
- Sacred Books
- Science Fiction
- Science & Technology
- Self-Help
- Social Sciences
- Symbolism
- Theatre & Drama
- Theology
- Travel & Explorations
- War & Military
- Women
- Yoga
- *Plus Much More!*

We kindly invite you to view our catalog list at:
http://www.kessinger.net

RELIGION AND PSYCHOLOGY

BY WILLIAM BROWN

Wilde Reader in Mental Philosophy in the University of
Oxford ; Hon. Consulting Psychologist and Lecturer on
Medical Psychology, Bethlem Royal Hospital, London ;
Psychotherapist to King's College Hospital, London.

CONTENTS

PAGE

1. Psychological Methods in the Study of Religion . . 303

2. Suggestion and Faith 312

3. Mysticism 320

I. Psychological Methods in the Study of Religion

In considering how far psychology can throw light upon religion, it is desirable to set out from some general conception of what Religion is. Religion itself is a state of mind, a mental attitude towards the universe : it is an attitude which we take up towards the totality of existence. Now there are many different attitudes with which we may face existence. We may meet it with a question, as we do in asking what it is, what is the universe and what are we as parts of the universe. We may endeavour to get to know the universe, and in some mysterious way we do succeed to some extent in understanding it, as a general system of physical and mental forces. Or again, we may enjoy the universe as a work of art or a collection of works of art. We may appreciate the beauty of the scenery and other things about us. We may deplore ugliness which we find intermingled with that beauty. Thirdly, we may face existence from the point of view of duty, of what should be done, or more adequately, in the light of the idea of the Good. There are, then, these three general all-inclusive attitudes towards the universe : (1) a cognitive attitude, based upon the desire to know ; (2) an aesthetic attitude, based upon the desire to appreciate, to do full justice to the beauty of existence, and perhaps to play some little part in adding to that beauty, if the individual is an artist ; (3) an ethical attitude, based upon the desire to achieve the highest good possible in individual conduct.

Is there a further general attitude remaining over after these three attitudes have, I won't say received adequate satisfaction, but at any rate have discovered their appropriate fields of activity ? There seems to be such a field in the experience of personal relationship towards the universe as that upon which we completely depend. That is, there is an attitude of complete dependence upon the universe which is distinct from the cognitive, aesthetical, and ethical attitudes. This attitude was first singled out by Schleiermacher as the essential element in the religious consciousness. But if we analyse the situation psychologically, we find that there are other forms of experience in this attitude besides the experience of complete dependence, and these additional forms of experience have been well analysed and described by Professor Rudolf Otto in his recent book, " The Idea of the Holy " (" Das Heilige "). He shows very clearly that the feeling of dependence which is characteristic of the religious attitude is not one of merely causal dependence, not the experience of being a link in a series of causal processes, just a link on the chain of causation, but something still more thorough-going, the experience of what he calls creature-hood, that " It is God that hath made us and not we ourselves." We have been made by Him and so we are completely dependent upon Him in that sense, made by Him and therefore entirely in His power. And then there are the further feelings called out in our mind by that idea, the feeling of His infinite power, the feeling of the tremendous, of complete otherness, something entirely different from ourselves, the feeling of mysteriousness, of majesty, and of fascination in which fear and attraction are blended.

I am taking this particular line of approach to the problem, because it seems to me that in this way one can avoid so much of the arguing in a circle that is to be found in the historical approach, which is the usual so-called scientific approach to the question of the religious sentiment. Usually, we find introductory chapters on lower forms of religious observance, and we have explained to us how, in the course of evolution, there must have been a pre-religious state in which magic figured largely. In magic the individual attempted to get his own way with the powers around him by spells and incantations, and then later, as a result of failure, relative or absolute, of these spells, the individual turned from the attitude of magic to the attitude of prayer or supplication, and at the same time passed from polytheism to a form of monotheism. Along this line of thought, according to this natural history of re-ligion, one is given the impression that the higher forms of religious feeling and religious insight are simply products of lower forms of mental activity : religion has grown out of forms of consciousness that could not themselves be called religious. In a similar way, attempts have been made to explain knowledge as a development out of mental processes that are not themselves knowledge, the sense of duty as a development out of simpler mental processes not themselves involving the feeling of obligation, the appreciation of beauty as a development out of forms of mental experience not themselves involving beauty, but merely sensations of pleasure and displeasure. Such an approach to the problem of religion is inadequate, if not positively misleading. In considering the subject, we need to take a broader view. At the commencement, at any rate, we must start from a philosophical outlook rather than a merely psychological one. What is first in philosophy is last in science.

For the merely psychologically minded, progress in the science of knowledge, and in the other mental sciences too, might be presumed to mean a greater and greater restriction of the field of religion, and to some minds, at any rate, an ultimate explaining away of religious experience. It was fear that in the beginning of things created the gods, and through knowledge the scope of that fear has been ever more and more reduced. But what has really happened is rather this. Starting with a general attitude towards life, in which these various values of experience were not distinct from one another, where science and religion, ethics and aesthetics, were all mingled together, the development of knowledge and civilisation has brought about a gradual separating out of these attitudes—each attitude, as I said at the beginning, has achieved its own general sphere of reference and of fact—and yet we find, after the claims of what may be called the profane sciences have been met, that there is something left over—namely, the distinctively religious experience itself.

It is true that this religious experience has been specially closely associated with ethical experience in the course of mental development in the individual as well as in the race ; forms of worship and religious appreciation have been linked up more and more closely with moral valuations, so that in the higher religions it is impossible to think away moral predicates from the conception of the Divine. Yet there remain non-rational in addition to these rational moral predicates, characteristics of the Divine which we can merely indicate in words—non-rational types of feeling, such as the feeling of dependence, of otherness, of the mysterious, the tremendous, etc., already referred to. These have their lower as well as their higher forms. In lower forms they appear in various species of superstition, fear of ghosts, the feeling of uncanniness, the otherness of the miraculous or the supernatural. These feelings gradually alter under the influence of increased knowledge, but do not disappear entirely. They are purified and pass from a lower

x

to a higher form, and so in spite of all the progress of scientific thought there remains this particular mental attitude which has been called by Professor Otto the " numinous," (from the Latin word *numen*, divinity), and he claims, and I think rightly, that in this attitude we have a definite form of experience and a definite way of experiencing reality ; not just a feeling that may vary from one person to another, that may come and go and perhaps disappear entirely with further mental development, but a way of experiencing reality on the same level with the cognitive attitude—the attitude of knowing reality—and the other attitudes which I have enumerated.　The task of Psychology is partly to do full justice to this mental attitude by analysing it in as detailed a way as possible, partly to link it up with other forms of experience not generally recognised as religious.

A great deal of work has been done by the method of the questionnaire, in which the investigator sends out a series of questions about their religious feelings to a large number of people. One of the first to adopt this course was Professor Starbuck in America, and in the first great book on the psychology of religion, by Professor William James, Professor Starbuck's results were largely used.　James here marshals the evidence, and sums up the characteristics of the religious life (independently of the discrepancies of creed) as including the following beliefs : " (1) That the visible world is part of a more spiritual universe from which it draws its chief significance ; (2) That unison or harmonious relation with that higher universe is our true end ; (3) That prayer or inner communion with the spirit thereof—be that spirit ' God ' or ' law '—is a process wherein work is really done, and spiritual energy flows in and produces effects, psychological or material, within the phenomenal world " (" Varieties of Religious Experience," p. 485).

It also becomes clear from the evidence that the phenomenon of *conversion* is a fundamental process in the religious life.　Conversion may be defined as a change of general mental attitude from the merely naturalistic attitude towards life to a definitely spiritual attitude.　The individual finds the world so full of strange and wonderful things that his mind is at first mainly occupied with getting to understand and appreciate it in a profane way, but he discovers that this is not sufficient to give him true happiness.　In spite of his most earnest endeavours to adjust himself to his physical and social environment and to be true to an ethical ideal, a feeling of insufficiency weighs upon his mind, and produces depression from which he struggles to free himself. Peace may come in one way or another, and the process of passing from such a state of conflict and strain to a state of harmony and peace is the process of conversion. Among certain religious sects conversion is striven after along definite lines. The sense of insufficiency and sin is emphasised in the prospective convert. He is encouraged to struggle hard against his difficulties, to face them, and to realise them as fully as possible. He passes through a state of intense mental anguish, and then suddenly reaches a state of calm and peace. But in another class of individuals who take religious life just as seriously, such sudden conversion may not occur. Yet I do not think that we can say that conversion as such is absent, and I am inclined to believe that conversion in its general sense of turning from the merely naturalistic attitude towards life to a more spiritual attitude occurs in every case, but in many cases it may occur slowly and gradually, as a process of healthy growth. Cases of sudden conversion are often to some extent pathological. I do not mean that the conversion itself is pathological, but that the conditions and consequences may be in part pathological. The strain and stress of mental conflict may produce temporary disturbance of functioning of the nervous system, and in that way give rise to experiences that are not in every respect normal religious experiences ;—depression, hallucinations, and even temporary delusions that show very close resemblance to the depression, hallucinations, and delusions met with in mental patients quite independently of their religious life.

The feeling of peace and relief may be partly explained on the psychological side as a transition from a state of division of the self, where one part of the self is fighting against another, to a state of unification and harmony. In this transition from division to unification a certain amount of energy is liberated which as a surplus allows all mental processes to occur more readily and freely, producing a feeling of happiness. This is an extremely crude theory, in terms of physiology and psychology, and certainly cannot be accepted as a fully adequate account of the process. The truth is that, so long as we speak merely as psychologists, we are tending to leave out the truly religious attitude altogether. Again, I can only illustrate by the analogy of knowledge. So far as we treat knowledge psychologically, we describe what goes on in the individual mind as a sequence of individual processes which if taken by itself would actually explain away knowledge. It would leave us without that conviction of the *validity* of our knowledge which is such an essential part of it. And so it is with religious experience. Psychologically, in the very effort that we make to describe religious experience as a sequence of mental processes in the individual's mind, we are invalidating that experience. We might, indeed, say that we are making an experiment, we are seeing how far we *can* explain the religious experience of the individual in terms of that individual's own antecedent experience without reference to anything beyond, that we are for the time being putting aside transcendence, because directly we assume that the individual is in touch with an existence outside him, we are passing beyond psychology. All that psychology does is to describe as accurately and fully as possible what goes on in his mind.

Moreover, psychology, like other sciences, is committed to the principle of parsimony, the principle of " Occam's razor," to use as few hypotheses as possible and to explain experience as fully as possible in terms of the most general hypotheses ; and this brings me to the use made of the doctrine of the subconscious or subliminal self, and in more recent years to the doctrine of the unconscious, to explain or explain away religious experience. Following up the hints of resemblance of certain startling religious experiences to certain pathological experiences, the attempt was made by James to fill up the gap, or to soften down the suddenness of the transition in the individual mind from the state of depression and sinfulness to a state of redemption, by an appeal to processes assumed to go on below the threshold of consciousness, in the subliminal. In the case of sudden conversion, for example, the theory was that the individual's consciousness seemed to remain on a merely naturalistic plane of existence, with a naturalistic outlook on life ; in the depths of his mind, however, a change was going on, other considerations were being weighed, other motives were getting their way, a subsidiary self was being developed, a set of mental tendencies which gained in strength and at last broke through into consciousness, and just before breaking through produced a feeling of intense strain and depression. When, however, it had broken through, it was able to combine with what it found there, modifying it, transforming it entirely, so that the individual felt a new man, as if he were born again. James himself goes further, and suggests that it may well be that the individual conscious mind comes into relation with the Deity through the intermediation of the subconscious mind. The changes in the conscious mind, in the direction of a more satisfactory religious attitude, may be produced through the intermediation of the subconscious, and in this way prayer may receive its answer. Influences may reach us through the dreamy subliminal which in the hubbub of waking life might pass us by.

From the scientific point of view, one would criticise such a theory as this, because it is not thorough-going enough. If you bring in the conception of the subliminal, and use it as an hypothesis, it is your duty as scientists to press that hypothesis to the utmost. Although James did not do this, it has been done by later writers, and in modern times we find a number of enthusiastic psychologists who look to the unconscious for an explanation of all these phenomena, but who, one cannot help feeling, have at the back of their minds the idea that they can only truly rely upon religious experience if it proves recalcitrant to this method. On the one hand, they will reject the supernatural, in the sense of the belief in a spiritual universe as distinct from the ordinary universe in space and time, because all the possibilities of explanation in terms of what goes on in the individual mind have not been exhausted, and yet, on the other hand, they are quite certain that these possibilities of explanation will never be exhausted. To all intents and purposes they are sceptics with regard to the validity of religious experience. The present situation of the psychology of religion is very similar to the situation as regards knowledge at the time when Locke, Berkeley, and Hume were writing. They were endeavouring to get to know what knowledge meant, their aim was to understand knowledge, to know about human understanding, but they used a predominantly psychological method, and although that psychological method increased their knowledge of psychology, it only made the central problem of knowledge more apparent, and it remained for Kant to show how completely they had failed to do justice to the science of knowledge. In the same way, at the present day and during the last twenty years, psychologists have approached the question of the validity of religious experience along psychological lines, not always realising that, by the very method they have adopted, they are challenging or denying that validity. In other words, just as psychology as such cannot do justice to the validity of knowledge, psychology cannot do justice to the validity of religion. Of course, it is open to every one to pass beyond the psychological to the philosophical line of explanation, and it is just as essential to do that in the problem of religion as it is in the problems of ethics, aesthetics, and epistemology.

Having emphasised this side of the question, we can with a clearer conscience proceed to apply psychological methods and observations to religious experience, although at every step in our argument we shall find it necessary to supplement psychology with philosophy. I am thinking at the moment of the attempts made by certain members of the psycho-analytic school to explain away the main facts of the Christian religion in terms of concepts borrowed from pathological psychology. One continental writer, who does not himself belong to the Christian faith, explains the central or main tenets of the Christian doctrine in terms of " projection " and " regression." He contends that the Christian attitude towards life is an infantile attitude that arises as a result of the individual's complete failure to grapple with the mystery of exist-ence. The individual tries to face the facts of reality, fails, and regresses towards more infantile modes of adaptation. Not being able to see adequate security among the forces of nature around him, he steps back to the mental attitude he had when a young child, of implicit faith in the power and goodness of his parents, in the modified form of a belief in a beneficent Deity. His belief in the Divine is simply this infantile feeling, which may surge up even in spite of himself. Again, his intense desire to conserve or preserve his values, logical, ethical, and aesthetical, all those things that make life for him worth living, may be so strong that it pro-duces a sort of hallucinatory fulfilment. It produces a feeling in him that it is fulfilled, that everything is all right, that we are safe in God's hands. Just to illustrate the kind of explanation proffered nowadays, we may mention that another psycho-analyst undertakes to explain the feeling of original sin in terms of the Oedipus complex. The individual has a bad conscience because in his childhood he felt a strong affection for one of his parents, and hatred and jealousy towards the other, which he repressed, and, as a result of repression, there arose feelings of sympathy and bad conscience. These were projected outwards and formed the basis of the systematic doctrines of the Fatherhood of God, the Atonement, etc.[1]

We can meet these arguments in two ways : one theoretical and the other practical. Theoretically, we can say that they are guilty of what Aristotle called a μετάβασις εἰς ἄλλο γένος,— the fallacy of explaining the facts of one science in terms of the concepts of another—of explaining the normal mind in terms of the abnormal, without first giving an adequate theory of the distinction between normal and abnormal. An analogous situation exists in the neighbouring science of physiology. No one would explain physiological change in terms of pathology. Physiology benefits by knowledge gained from pathology. Pathology also clearly gains enormously from the knowledge of physiology. But the two sciences are quite distinct. Clearly pathology is in the main subsidiary to physiology. The second line of attack is the more satisfactory one of actual experience. According to one's experiences of the pathological processes of projection and regression and the influence of the Oedipus complex in a patient, these are usually diminished or eliminated by a course of psycho-analysis. If, therefore, the typical religious attitude towards life is explicable in these terms, the religious consciousness would be altered by analysis in the direction of elimination. One would expect, according to this theory, that deep analysis would leave the patient less religious than he was before. My own experience has been the exact opposite of this. After an analysis (for scientific purposes) by a leading psycho-analyst extending over ninety-two hours, my religious convictions were stronger than before, not weaker. The analysis had indeed a purifying effect upon my religious feelings, freeing them from much that was merely infantile and supported by sentimental associations or historical accidents. But the ultimate result has been that I have become more convinced than ever that religion is the most important thing in life and that it is essential to mental health. The need of forms and ceremonies is another matter, far less fundamental. In many patients whom I have myself analysed I have found a similar result. Although mere

---

[1] Although psychological factors of this kind, among others, may contribute their share to crude religious emotion, to use them to explain away the essential characteristics of religious experience would be to " pour away the baby with the bath-water."

emotionalism and religiosity is diminished, the essentially religious outlook on life remains unimpaired.

2. SUGGESTION AND FAITH

We may now consider in more detail the psychological factors at work in bringing us into relationship with the Divine, and there occurs at once to the therapeutic mind the problem of the general nature of faith, and its relation to suggestion. The modern psycho-therapeutic doctrine of suggestion was a direct development from the rather extreme views of Christian Scientists of thirty or forty years ago. So-called faith cures were produced by Mrs. Eddy and her followers supported by the enthusiasm they had for this line of thought, and many medical and other psychologists who investigated the matter came to the conclusion that, for the most part, the cures could be explained in terms of suggestion. It therefore behoves us to understand as clearly as possible what is meant by suggestion and the theory and practice of suggestion-treatment, and the bearing it has upon faith and other forms of religious experience. Suggestion may be defined as the acceptance of an idea by the mind, especially by the so-called subconscious mind, independently of adequate logical grounds for such acceptance. It is an instance of ideo-motor action. The idea is placed before the mind, or rather, aroused vividly in the mind, when the mind is in a state where opposing and conflicting ideas have no chance of making themselves felt ; whereupon this implanted or elicited idea tends to realise itself. It takes a certain time in doing so, known as the " latent period." In a simple case of suggestion, then, the mind of the individual is in a passive state, free from contradictory or conflicting ideas, receptive, ready to allow the suggested idea or ideas to be aroused in full force. The idea has a tendency to pass over into action, to bring about its own realisation, in so far as it is not interfered with by conflicting ideas. Favouring factors in suggestion are a state of general passivity, muscular as well as sensory, combined with concentration upon some neutral idea. We find in psycho-therapeutic practice, when we wish to produce benefit by suggestion, that our best results are obtained if we get the patient into a passive state, when the muscles are relaxed, a state not so much of attention as what is called by Baudouin *contention*—a state of concentration without effort. We eliminate effort by requesting the patient to relax his muscles, and we encourage concentration by giving him something to concentrate upon. The mind, although passive, is not in a state of distraction. It is narrowed down upon some very general idea, preferably upon the idea of sleep, and if in that state an idea is aroused in the mind, an idea of some change in the patient's bodily and mental condition, that idea tends to realise itself to its utmost possible extent. A convenient time for giving suggestion is before rest at night. At that time the patient has relinquished all his interests in matters of the day, he is more able to get really peaceful and relaxed, and the background of his mind, the so-called subconscious mind, is more accessible to outside influences. In referring to the subconscious in this way, one seems to be speaking rather metaphorically, as if the subconscious were a sort of occult force. It is not exactly that, but rather a class concept, including mental tendencies which are not clearly present in consciousness. Indeed, it is those tendencies not clearly present in consciousness that are most important in suggestion treatment, because those which are clearly conscious have appropriate ideas linking them up with other conscious tendencies. The mind, so far as it is conscious, is alert and acts therefore according to more or less rational motives. Suggestion to the conscious mind has usually little effect—it is transitory if it takes effect at all. Persuasion, which uses rational arguments, is the more appropriate and effective influence in this sphere. Suggestion is a kind of affirmation, it is rightly addressed to the subconscious, to the fundamental tendencies of the mind that are not directly represented in consciousness.

The question then arises, What is the relation between suggestion, as we have thus explained it, and faith ? The following example may throw some preliminary light upon this problem. A year or two ago I was treating a boy of thirteen for some disturbing nervous symptoms which interfered with his life at school, and which he was most anxious to get rid of, by means of suggestion (after a preliminary analysis of the conditions in which the illness began). The first two or three hours of suggestion treatment, during each of which he lay passive on a couch, receiving suggestions from me every five minutes or so, seemed to produce very little if any effect, till about the fourth treatment, when he suddenly burst into tears, and said in a voice charged with emotion, " Now I really do believe that it is going to be all right, I feel absolutely certain about it." From that moment his symptom (enuresis) disappeared, and he became permanently well. In this case we have an interesting illustration of a transition from suggestion to a state of faith. In suggestion the mind is passively stimulated to produce an idea, and then this idea in its turn realises itself, because it has no competitors, it works automatically, by its own momentum as it were. In faith, on the other hand, one finds a state of mind which is essentially active ; as William James said, there is a will to believe, it is a definite assertion or affirmation of an active mind. The whole mind is active and the experience is accompanied by an emotion which is something of the nature of volition, a determination to give oneself up completely to the idea for some reason or other. It may be just in order to get rid of a symptom, or for the sake of higher development of the mind—a belief in the possibility of such higher development.

Intermediate between suggestion and faith is auto-suggestion, where the individual gives suggestions to himself. In auto-suggestion he is passive, he thinks of sleep, he gets for a moment or two into a comatose state, almost free from all activity and yet in a state of concentration, and then, in some wonderful way, he is able to present to himself the idea, or bring up before himself the idea, of what he wants, the change he wishes to bring about in his mind or body. He, as we say, affirms this idea to himself, that *e.g.* at night he will sleep well, and wake up feeling much better and free from the stammer, or nervousness, or difficulty of concentration, or whatever it may be, that he will be able to concentrate well, to remember well, to feel cheerful and happy ; and experience shows us that beneficial results definitely follow. By perseverance in the use of this method the patient can often transform his whole outlook upon life. I look upon auto-suggestion as a bad term. It is really something more akin to faith than to suggestion. It is the cultivation of a special active attitude of mind, an assertion of health and of faith in its possibility—a particular kind of healthy-mindedness. If you treat yourself by auto-suggestion, you get benefit so far as you can make it depend upon the extent to which you can really believe and affirm to yourself the gospel of health, that health is more real than disease ; that so far as the will of God goes, He wills health rather than disease. With such a crude belief results actually do follow.

In dealing with these problems, which are, of course, really extremely difficult, it is necessary to take facts first and look for theories afterwards. We can say as a fact that suggestion produces results, that auto-suggestion produces still more permanent results, and that, if genuine faith is aroused, the most astounding results of a permanent nature may be produced. In this sequence, looked at psychologically, we see that the transition is from passivity to activity, that faith as such is a form of volition, and that auto-suggestion as such is not in conflict with volition, as M. Coué and his followers have wrongly contended ; it is simply a completion of volition. The so-called law of reversed effort, which Coué and his followers have made famous, may be expressed in this form: "When the will and the imagination are in conflict, the imagination always wins." The conclusion would seem to be that imagination is stronger than will ; but in the French the word *vouloir*, though sometimes meaning will, often means wish, and, so far as one can make out in Coué's own brief writings, he is thinking really of wish rather than of will. If there is a wish on the one hand and imagination on the other, the imagination-result is more likely to occur than the wish-result ; indeed, the situation is one of frustrated will. The process of wishing is on the road towards volition or will, but it has not yet reached the final stage of volition. In that transition from wishing to willing or volition, the imagination, lighted up and intensified by fear or some other disturbing emotion, slips in as it were, gets the lead, and prevents the wish becoming the will. Imagination then wins because the will has not been completed. On the other hand, that which has been called auto-suggestion, and which I think is a definite attitude of mind akin to faith, is a process of complete volition, turning mere wish into will by adequate control of the imagination.

This will become clear if we take an example. A patient suffering from a fear of open spaces, called technically agoraphobia may be unable to walk a hundred yards down a wide street by himself or to cross it. As soon as he attempts to start on his journey, his heart palpitates, he becomes breathless, tends to hug the wall, becomes less and less able to move, is glued to the spot, and has to give up and return home. Such a patient may be encouraged by his relatives and friends to pull himself together and to make a real effort, and may be told that if he makes an adequate effort he will succeed in getting over this difficulty. But he finds, on the contrary, that the greater the effort the worse the situation becomes, the harder he tries the less he succeeds. This seems to be a situation akin to that summed up in Coué's law of reversed effort ; on the one side, the will to walk alone, on the other side, the imagination, the fear, that he will not succeed ; and in this conflict imagination wins. But, on looking more closely into the situation, one realises that there is no complete volition here. The patient is ill, his mental processes do not enable him to will completely in this particular situation. Why, is a matter to be discovered in other ways, through deep analysis— deep analysis will show why he is unable to will to cross the street. In his attempt to will to walk along or to cross the street, the feeling of effort becomes more vivid and more intense, but it remains a mere wish or suggestion. Opposed to this effortful wish to cross the street, one finds the idea or suggestion of failure accompanied by the fear of failure. In this conflict the suggestion of failure accompanied by the emotion of fear obviously will win, as against the suggestion, unaccompanied by any strong emotion, that he will cross the street. This so-called law of reversed effort is thus merely a simple illustration of conflict between one suggestion and another, or between one " imagination " and another. If this is so, what do we mean by will ? We mean a wish or desire, accompanied by the judgement, affirmation, or belief that we shall fulfil the desire from our own resources, so far as in us lies,—that we shall realise the desire because we desire it. In cases like that of agoraphobia [1] the object of the psychotherapist is to train the patient's will, so that one disagrees with Coué, and, instead of saying that a re-education of the will is useless, one rather points out that the patient has not achieved complete volition in this situation, and that he has to learn to will, after first discovering the cause of his incomplete volition by self-analysis or (much more effectively) by deep analysis carried out by the physician. In these cases mere suggestion as a passive thing is extremely ineffective. One may produce temporary alleviation by calming the patient's mind, and discouraging spasmodic effort and diminishing the tendency to intensify the symptoms by effort ; but the patient quickly falls back to the original state, because the cause is still there. The truth is, he has no faith in that particular treatment, nor in his power to cross the street, and there is reason for this lack of faith. In some cases one finds deep down in the

---

[1] So far as the agoraphobia is a manifestation of " anxiety neurosis " it is physically caused, and is to be treated by advice on sex-hygiene.

mind a fear of fainting ; he has fainted on some previous occasion, and so he has lost confidence in himself ; he feels he will be right away from all aid, so the mere sight of an open space arouses this subconscious idea, his heart beats rapidly, and the initial stages of a fainting attack set in with this feeling of anxiety, a feeling that he is " glued to the spot."

If, then, suggestion and faith are distinct, in what way can we indicate their relationship more clearly than we have already done ?   From the theoretical point of view, I think we can say that suggestion is ultimately always dependent upon some form or other of faith, and not conversely.   The patient may not be conscious of faith, he may respond to suggestion, and suggestion may be given in a mechanical way.   He may have no conscious faith in the method, but he finds that the method benefits him.   If one analyses him, however, one discovers that in his subconscious mind there is faith.   The relationship between suggestion and such a general (often subconscious) background of faith is similar to that between the empirical investigation of nature by scientists, and the general metaphysical principle of the uniformity of nature, within the domain of knowledge. A scientist would not be able to make a single step forward in his investigations or theories about the universe unless he had that belief in the uniformity of nature—that A remains A unless and until it is altered by some other factor, that if A becomes B there is some reason for it in the intrusion of further factors. Unless he holds this metaphysical belief in the uniformity of nature, he is unable to form hypotheses, and by their means advance in scientific knowledge.   His individual generalisations from facts of experience are based upon this belief.   Similarly an individual benefits by suggestion treatment along special lines because of his more general belief or faith in the universe.   The individual may not consciously hold such a faith, but somewhere in his mind there is that faith, the belief in a friendliness somewhere, and if he is completely lacking in it, then he will be completely inaccessible to therapeutic suggestion.   Actually, in the case of everyone, there is the tendency, the readiness to believe in friendliness outside— based upon early childhood experiences and inherited tendencies. This again brings us back from the point of view of suggestion and faith to the more fundamental problem of " deep " analysis.

Some psycho-analysts consider that the facts of suggestion, of faith-healing, etc., are explicable in terms of early experiences within the bosom of the family, in terms of the Oedipus complex and psychological reactions thereto. The theory is a very complicated one and cannot be dealt with in detail here.[1] One may, however, consider it in its most formal aspect, and point out that the whole question of faith in terms of infantile experience is based upon an original postulate. It is not necessarily based upon facts at all ; facts may later on be discovered to support the special details of the theory, but the general theory has its real basis elsewhere, in the *postulate* that whatever is in the mind can be explained in terms of previous experience. It is the postulate of determinism. Some psychologists may think that determinism is on the road to being proved through the further development of psychology. That, of course, is reasoning in a circle, because what we do in psychology is to look for causes of the various effects that we see, on the basis of the postulate of determinism. In philosophy there is the fundamental principle of sufficient reason (Leibnitz), the principle that there is always a sufficient reason why anything should happen rather than not happen. Determinism looks for the sufficient reason in any particular case always in what has already occurred. We therefore know beforehand, however rapidly deep analysis may develop—and it is developing rapidly every year now—we know beforehand that it will seem to restrict ever more and more the doctrine of the freedom of the will. The further psychology advances, the less will the idea of freedom, or of spontaneity of the mind, be apparent. But the very fact that we can predict this shows that it is not the result of psychological advance. Psychology cannot either prove or disprove determinism.

More cautious psychologists adopt the doctrine of self-determinism. They must adopt some form of determinism if they are to be psychologists at all, in order to link up and co-ordinate mental events within a wider system. But they take as their system not the antecedent processes of the mind only, but the entire mind right up to the present moment. The test of a determinist doctrine is the power of prediction, and, in the case of mental process, prediction is impossible unless we know every moment of the person's life right up to the moment when the action which we are supposed to be predicting occurs. The act is then completely

---

[1] See especially S. Freud : *Totem and Tabu*, *Group Psychology and the Analysis of the Ego*, and *Das Ich und das Es*.

determined because it is determined by his entire self. This is a doctrine of self-determinism, rather than determinism, because it is determinism within a self which is growing, and which acts as a whole. What we mean by freedom is the power of the mind of the individual acting as a whole. A person is free and is acting freely when he is most himself in carrying out an action. The kind of action that to us seems impulsive action, where we feel out of ourselves, out of our mind, and we wonder later on however we could have done such a thing, such action is not free. So far as conduct is the outcome of the whole mind working in its unity, so far it is self-determined, and free in the only sense in which we can understand freedom.

Although one may seem to have deviated along another line of thought, and to have left the question of faith, it is of significance for the problem of faith, because faith is such an affirmation of the entire mind. Someone has defined faith as a readiness to trust and to follow the noblest hypothesis ; it is an act of self-assertion, one decides to be on the side of the angels, takes one's side in the battle of existence, for battle it is. Ideally at least, it should represent an attitude of the entire mind, but it may often be not so complete. It may often be rather a momentary mood, and so far as it is that, it may be followed by a relapse. Here the vexed question of spiritual healing arises. The process of spiritual healing is a process of arousing faith, the faith state, and that faith state may have different degrees of rationality, which is the same thing as saying that it may extend over a smaller or larger area of the self, and if it is limited to a small part of the self, it may mislead the individual instead of helping him. One reason why many of us are very doubtful of the wisdom of spiritual-healing services is that, for many who attend such services, it is an appeal to superficial emotion and to primitive credulity. There is the tendency to intensify that hysterical condition of mind from which many of the patients are already suffering. In some cases there may be a disappearance of hysterical symptoms and apparent cure, but only at the expense of replacement by another symptom—namely, reliance upon a quasi-miraculous possibility, the expectation of getting something for nothing, as it were, of getting direct gifts without full appreciation of corresponding demands upon personality. Mass-suggestion may produce startling results of a temporary and superficial kind, but individual treatment is more likely to produce deep and lasting benefit.

The whole question of spiritual healing is one of extreme difficulty, and awaits further medical and psychological investigation. But among its more obvious dangers we cannot overlook the danger of intensifying the hysterical or the infantile attitude towards life that many neurotic patients have, and the danger of disappointment and of a set-back to their faith in the case of those who receive no benefit.

3. MYSTICISM

We now come to a consideration of what is probably the most important form of religious experience—namely, mystical experience—to which all other religious feelings seem to lead up. The mystical experience is an experience of apparently direct union with the Divine. It is a form of meditation which leads the soul up to divinity. In this mental state the person may lose the feeling of individuality, and may seem to pass beyond the limitations of space and time. When he endeavours to describe his experience he can only express it in negatives. He can say what the experience is not, but he is quite unable to say what it is. One of the greatest authorities on mysticism is Saint Theresa, and her own experience and general theory are summed up in that important book, " The Interior Castle," in which she describes various stages of union with the Divine. In almost every form of religion in the world we find similar experiences described, although there are individual differences. Leaving aside these differences, we find quite enough identity to convince us that, just as religious feeling itself is a special mental attitude towards life and a sort of knowledge of reality, so here in mysticism we have its central core, the most characteristic way in which our religious knowledge comes to us. If only it were universal, there would be no further trouble about the matter. Unfortunately, so many people protest that they are unable to verify the occurrence of mystical experience in themselves ; this is a serious difficulty in the way of its significance or validity, though not destroying its interest for psychology.

Before considering this matter further, it would be well to mention certain types of experience that are analogous to the mystical experience, but that otherwise are not regarded as of special religious value or importance. In the first place, there is the peculiar feeling of joy, exultation, or rapture that may accompany certain sensory experiences. Certain bars of music and phrases of poetry seem to have a quite irrational appeal that cannot be explained in terms of the actual associations of the sounds or meaning of the words, but apparently touch some hidden chord in the mind, and thereby stir the soul deeply. Muscular and kinaesthetic sensations sometimes arouse a similar feeling. Well-ordered muscular activity may often induce a feeling of unity with nature. On a beautiful spring morning, when away from one's fellow men in the fields, one may be suddenly overtaken with a feeling of the direct continuity of one's own life with the life of nature. One looks with different eyes upon the scenery and welcomes it as a part of one's self, or rather, as something infinitely greater than one's self in which one is merged. This feeling may be intensified in special circumstances, as *e.g.* when riding, in which no doubt sympathy with the horse as well as the muscular exercise play their part. We might perhaps explain these, often extremely pleasant, experiences as a sort of reversion to an earlier and more primitive form of consciousness, when we were less aware of our own individuality and its problems : when we were more in touch with the animals and plants around us, and felt our kinship with them more vividly. Since it is not an experience constantly present, when it does come it comes with a special vividness, as intensified pleasure, which is not surprising ; it is normal and healthy, not pathological. Communion is in general a healthy form of experience. It is the feeling of isolation from nature, animate and inanimate, which is the terrible thing, and which we find in such pronounced form among some of our mentally deranged patients.

Secondly, there are the mental states sometimes produced by anaesthetics—the so-called " anaesthetic revelation." Under the influence of alcohol, ether, chloroform, and especially of nitrous oxide gas, many people get extraordinary feelings of deepened insight into the meaning of things. They may come out of the anaesthetic with the conviction that they have solved the riddle of the universe, and suffer great disappointment because all they can find in their minds at the moment of awakening are some doggerel rhymes that have no significance whatever. Then again, a similar mystical experience can come over one in conditions of self-hypnosis. If one lies passive on a couch with the eyes closed and all voluntary muscles relaxed, and breathes slowly and deeply in order to increase that relaxation, one may feel oneself slipping away from the world of clear consciousness, losing the feeling of orientation and of sensitivity in the limbs. The body seems to be floating in the air, and later on one may feel that one does not possess a body at all.   In this state, one seems to become depersonalised, as it were, absorbed in the " all," into the soul of the universe.   One attains to what has been called cosmic consciousness.

Now can we find any identical factor in these various experiences ?   In all except those accompanying muscular exercise, in the anaesthetic revelation, auto- and hetero-hypnosis, etc., one characteristic seems to be the abolition of the motor tendency.   In a normal man who goes about his affairs with eyes wide open and mind alert, there is a definite adjustment of muscular activity to the needs of the situation.   His muscles are tense and always ready to come into action, and his experience is essentially sensori-motor. It is probably this motor aspect of experience that intensifies the feeling of personality, and if it is brought into abeyance with anaesthetics or special artificial modes of relaxation, the sense of personality disappears with it.   The individual is less conscious of the dividing lines between himself and the rest of the universe.

It is clear that, in mystical experiences proper, we ought to allow for the possible admixture of such experiences as these and discount them ; although it is more than doubtful whether we can say that all religious mystic experience should be explained in terms of such cruder experiences.   Some scientists tend to criticise all these experiences as abnormal, because they involve a disturbance of the sensori-motor attitude towards life.   But this would be to make a very great assumption, an assumption analogous to the one we have already discussed in connection with determinism.   Such scientists map out a general system of explanation, and everything they find in that system they call scientific.   Everything not explained in terms of that system they attempt to explain as pathological, and in calling it pathological they deny the validity or importance of it.

An alternative explanation would be the following : it is very obvious that experience, as we know it, occurs and comes to us under the forms of space and time, because we are embodied minds, because we are limited, finite parts of the universe, and yet we have in us powers that can in some way lift us beyond these limits.   It seems quite clear that one such power is that of thought : another is the direct insight of aesthetic appreciation ; and religious experience in its mystical form may prove the greatest power of all in this direction.   When, in the mystical experience, we have the feeling of timelessness, it is quite conceivable that we *are* passing beyond the limits of time, and proving, to ourselves at any rate, that time is appearance and not reality, and that immortality is not something we have to wait for at the end of this life, but something we can and do achieve in varying degrees while still living this life. That has been the view of leading philosophers throughout the ages. We find Aristotle urging his readers, ἐφ' ὅσον ἐνδέχεται ἀθανατίζειν, to be immortal as far as possible, even in this life.

Thus we come to the tremendous metaphysical problem of the reality of time, which is, perhaps, the greatest metaphysical problem of the present day, and especially important to our point of view of personality. So long as we consider time as one of the conditions of individual experience, we are tied down to a certain theory of personality, which may easily be the wrong one. All psychological theories of personality, of course, are of this nature, and, to a great extent, they are for that reason rather depressing, because they emphasise the limits that we are all aware of. But in emphasising these limits they tend to make them much more complete and ultimate than they really are for us. Again, if we take physiological modes of thought in considering psychological problems, we are impressed by rates of rhythm of physiological processes. As physiological psychologists we may be impressed by experiments which show that estimation of time is most accurate with a certain rhythm and less accurate with shorter or longer rhythms, or again, that experience of succession has a lower limit of causation. In the background there may be the unspoken but fallacious assumption that the experience of succession is the same as, or at least runs parallel with, a succession of experiences; and again the further assumption that a succession of experiences runs parallel with a succession of physiological changes somewhere or other in the organism. It is easy to show by metaphysical argument that the conception of time as something ultimately real leads us to definite antinomies or contradictions, from which we cannot escape unless we agree to regard time as appearance and not reality. But we still find it extremely difficult to understand most aspects of experience, unless we do regard time as real. If we consider experience in detail, we see how much time contributes to the quality of that experience. So impressed was Bergson by this fact that he has taken time as the very stuff of which reality is made. He speaks of *durée réelle* as something which is ultimate, although he regards the time of mathematical physics and the other physical sciences as spatialised time. Of course, many of the goods and pleasures of life seem to be bound up with the time function. Time is essential even to such a good as the ethical good, the good will. A good action is one which is definitely and deliberately intended and carried out, and can only be carried out in the course of time. If one imagines time transcended, it is difficult to imagine any strictly moral action, or indeed any action at all. It is difficult to attribute the characteristics of morality, which is one of our three general values, to a timeless experience. In transcending time, one seems to transcend morality as such. In aesthetic experience time-lessness seems to be more possible. When we enjoy a picture, for the time being we feel ourselves out of time ; its artistic meaning is timeless. But then when we turn to music, another form of art, time appears to be of its essence, though even here we should not be too certain of this. We know there is an anecdote about Mozart, who, in speaking of one of his compositions, explains how he first had it in his head before he wrote it down. He heard all the notes together—*zusammen*. That was a wonderful experience, he said, the like of which he never heard again. In music there is a degree of transcendence of time : chords occur one after another, yet they have to combine in some way to give a feeling of harmony and melody, and one is conscious of what has gone before and what is about to come. One sees more meaning in the production the second time than the first, because one knows what is coming. So that one might say, with regard to music, that although the possibility of musical experience, and of the training of the ear, is bound up with the conditions of temporal sequence, yet the ultimate outcome when the trained ear appreciates the true inward meaning of music is something that is already on the way towards transcendence of time. As regards truth, it is quite clear that time is transcended—once true, always true. Although the proving to a class of school-boys that the three angles of a triangle are equal to two right angles takes time, and individual boys take varying lengths of time in gaining an adequate insight into that geometrical truth, once they have acquired the truth the insight is beyond time. Moreover, it was true before they began to consider it, and it will remain true after they have ceased to think of it. Truth, as truth, is certainly beyond time.

Finally, as regards religious experience, one feels that it is essential to this experience, if to any, that it should be beyond time. Although it may be conditioned by time, in that one gains a deeper and deeper insight into its truths through an experience that comes to one in the course of days, yet the experience itself takes us out of time and enables us to attain to a mystic attitude towards the universe, beyond any opportunism that acceptance of the reality of time can give. If we assume that time is completely real for us, that we are bound down in a time process, and that we do not transcend it at all, then our ultimate outlook upon reality is very depressing and unmeaning. Despite temporary improvements in the conditions of human life and the advance of physical science, this earth will eventually become uninhabitable, degeneration will come sooner or later to the race, to the physical side of things, so that in terms of matter and material change and temporal process there seems little room for ultimate hope. The life of the human race would really be " a tale told by an idiot, full of sound and fury, signifying nothing." But all the meaning we find in life is on the way towards a transcending of time. When we look towards a future life, we look not so much towards a life at some future time that some enthusiasts would like to prove and even describe for us, but to a life eternal, in which we pass beyond the conditions of the merely material, which of course is the temporal and spatial. We mean by matter something such that two portions of it cannot be in the same place at the same time—that is probably the best definition of matter which we can give. We can only think of matter in terms of space and time.

It is very significant that these various experiences that appear to transcend time, and also perhaps space, accompanied by disorientation in space and time, bring with them a diminution of feeling of individuality, so that at the end it looks as if we shall have to dismiss individuality with other aspects of existence as appearance and not reality. It is very doubtful whether we shall be able to preserve individuality as an ultimate value in the scheme of things ; it is a stepping-stone, no doubt, and, as far as we can see of existence in this life, there is a parallel process of individuation and inter-relation going on, so that really great individuals, great personalities, are those who have individualised their lives so that they are in closer communion with their fellows, rather than in isolation from them. In a way this is an absorption. The great statesman, the great man of action, the great scientist, is the person who is able to suppress his mere individuality in order that he may get a wider personality of the group or nation to which he belongs. The great statesman speaks for an entire nation, because he is able to understand the various needs of the individuals in it. He does not lose his personality thereby, he does not efface it, he makes it all the more real. On the other hand, the self-centred paranoiac who has to be shut up in an asylum is convinced of his own greatness, believes himself to be a reincarnation of Napoleon or of the Messiah, or even God himself, and, corresponding to his intense feeling of individuality and difference from others, we find a depressing bankruptcy in his mental make-up. The great scientist is he who keeps clear of fanaticism and crankiness by continuous moral effort, by effacing his own peculiarities, wishes, desires, and interests in the matter, in order to get as unbiased a view as possible of the facts. He has the greater task of effacing, not only the individuality of nationality, but of humanity itself, and yet in that process we cannot say that he is losing personality in the true sense of the word. Personality, then, ought to be distinguished from individuality. Individuality is a mere difference from others. Personality is a process of development, in which we have parallel processes of individuation and assimilation. The man of personality gives out to the world around him and also absorbs it in himself, identifying himself as far as possible with others and sympathising with their aims. Yet, in the end, even personality must go, because in the universe there is no room for merely separate persons. Ultimately there can only be one complete person, he who is completely self-sufficing, and he can only be completely self-sufficing if he has complete knowledge and power over his environment, and therefore he must extend throughout that environment, and must be the totality of Reality itself. The only complete person is the Absolute or God, and progress towards personality in individuals seems to be intellectual, along the path of reason. One can see it as a union, ever closer and deeper, with the spirit of the universe, as identification to a greater and greater extent with all that is highest in the universe, and that is the intellectual counterpart of what we mean by the mystical experience.

One might perhaps do more justice to this problem of the mystical by admitting that there is a lower and a higher form of mysticism. The lower form is on the plane of immediate feeling, unmediated by thought. Such is the experience of the athlete, the drug-addict, the devotee of self-hypnosis, the primitive artist in man. Here is an experience of direct union on a lower plane of feeling. Then thought discriminates, distinguishes subject from object, objects from one another, holds the mind apart from its object, and yet, in that process, links it up more and more closely with its object until, when its work is done as far as it can be done, again there arises a communion, a feeling that the subject-object relationship is being transcended, and this is the true, the highest mystical experience. It will include various types of experience. We will not identify it with religious mystical experience because we have already marked and separated that off from our other general attitudes towards the totality of things—the intellectual, the aesthetic, and the moral attitudes, and in each of these attitudes we find the higher form of mysticism. There remains the mysticism which may truly be called religious. But even that does not completely satisfy us, since we are left with four distinct things which we feel must in some way be unified. Actually, of course, they are unified in an all-inclusive experience, which is the real higher mystical experience, the mediation by thought of all the other attitudes, including the religious, so that just as the race began life in a primitive religious way, likewise at the end, after science and philosophy have done all that they can, the fundamental attitude is once more a religious attitude. An individual who is unable to get that attitude at all is to that extent incomplete. We sometimes find that such an individual is mentally sick, suffering from repressions which cut him off from it. With the removal of these repressions by analysis the experience may become once more possible to him.

It is only fair to mention here that one school of thought explains all these mystical experiences in terms of what is called Narcissism. In such experience there is a turning inwards of the mind upon itself, a drawing in of libido, a concentration of libido upon the self. An increase of Narcissism under certain conditions may bring with it a feeling of intense pleasure and of liberation, transcending time and space, although it is really a set-back, a regression, to an infantility of an extreme type. The actual evidence in support of so extreme a theory is quite inadequate, and against it may be set the general arguments of pp. 309, 318 above. But we should not overlook the rôle played by Narcissism in some forms of religious experience.[1]

[1] See, *e.g.*, Ernest Jones, " The Nature of Auto-suggestion," *British Journal of Medical Psychology*, vol. iii, 1923.

This is the end of this publication.

Any remaining blank pages are for our book binding requirements and are blank on purpose.

To search thousands of interesting publications like this one, please remember to visit our website at:

http://www.kessinger.net